The Big Story

OXFORD
UNIVERSITY PRESS

Great Clarendon Street, Oxford OX2 6DP

Oxford University Press is a department of the University of Oxford.
It furthers the University's objective of excellence in research, scholarship,
and education by publishing worldwide in

Oxford New York

Auckland Cape Town Dar es Salaam Hong Kong Karachi
Kuala Lumpur Madrid Melbourne Mexico City Nairobi
New Delhi Shanghai Taipei Toronto

With offices in

Argentina Austria Brazil Chile Czech Republic France Greece
Guatemala Hungary Italy Japan Poland Portugal Singapore
South Korea Switzerland Thailand Turkey Ukraine Vietnam

OXFORD and OXFORD ENGLISH are registered trade marks of
Oxford University Press in the UK and in certain other countries

© Oxford University Press 2010

ISBN: 978 0 19 424710 8 BOOK
ISBN: 978 0 19 463927 9 BOOK AND AUDIO PACK

No unauthorized photocopying

Printed in China

This book is printed on paper from certified and well-managed sources.

ACKNOWLEDGEMENTS

Illustrations by: Dylan Gibson

The publisher would like to thank the following for permission to reproduce photographs: Alamy Stock
Photo p6 (Big Ben/Anthony Wiles); Bridgeman Images pp40 (The Market and Fountain
of the Innocents, Paris, 1823, Chalon, John James/Musee de la Ville de Paris, Musee
Carnavalet, Paris, France), 41 (View of the Rialto at Venice, Canaletto/Collection of the Earl
of Leicester, Holkham Hall, Norfolk); Corbis pp19 (Cafe next to Rialto Bridge/Jon Hicks), 24
(Gondolier/Ric Ergenbright), 25 (Grand Canal from the Accademia Bridge/Sergio Pitamitz),
30 (The Grand Canal, Venice/Neil Emmerson/robertharding); OUP p12 (Skier/Photodisc).

DOMINOES

Series Editors: Bill Bowler and Sue Parminter

The Big Story

John Escott

Illustrated by Dylan Gibson

John Escott has written many books for readers of all ages, and particularly enjoys writing crime and mystery thrillers. He was born in the west of England, but now lives on the south coast. When he is not writing, he visits second-hand bookshops, watches videos of old Hollywood movies, and takes long walks along empty beaches. He has also written *The Wild West, A Pretty Face,* and *Kidnap!,* and retold *William Tell and Other Stories* for Dominoes.

OXFORD
UNIVERSITY PRESS

BEFORE READING

This is Rosie Doyle. She's a journalist and she lives in London. One day she goes to her office. What happens? Tick the boxes.

a At the office Rosie meets . . .

a
her editor

b
a thief

c
an art dealer

b She must find . . .

a
new work

b
a big story

c
lots of money

c She hears two Americans. One is . . .

a
a journalist

b
an art dealer

c
a thief

d They talk about . . .

a
lots of money

b
an expensive picture

c
work in New York

Rosie Doyle lives and works in London. She is a **journalist**. She writes for *The Record* **newspaper**.

journalist a person who writes stories for a newspaper

newspaper people read about things that happen every day in this

'I can't use this story, Rosie,' says the **editor**. 'It's old **news**. Bring me something new and exciting. Bring me a BIG story!' He looks at her. 'You're tired, Rosie. Take the afternoon off. Go and see a **film**, or something.'

'"A big story"! That's not easy to find,' Rosie thinks. 'But a film? Yes, that's a good **idea**.'

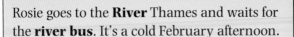

Rosie goes to the **River** Thames and waits for the **river bus**. It's a cold February afternoon.

---

editor the person who says which stories go in a newspaper

news when someone tells you something that is new

film moving pictures that tell a story

idea something that you think

river water that moves through the country in a long line

river bus people go from one place to another on a river in this

Rosie sits on the river bus and looks out at the city.

But a man and a woman in front of her on the river bus are not interested in the city's buildings. They are Americans. They talk, and Rosie begins to listen.

'Fifty thousand Euros, Ms Yardley,' the man says. 'I want fifty thousand Euros to get it.'
'I don't know, Lezardo—' Ms Yardley begins.
'It's **worth** half a million,' Lezardo says.
'Fifty thousand is nothing.'

worth how expensive something is

3

Rosie forgets about the film. It isn't important now. She listens carefully to the man and woman. 'Pierre Valmy's **chateau** is in the mountains,' Lezardo says. 'The job isn't easy. And it's **dangerous**.'

'All right,' Ms Yardley says. 'Fifty thousand. Bring it to Venice on Thursday afternoon. Two o'clock at the Rialto **Bridge**.'

Rosie gets off the river bus. The man and the woman are in front of her. The man walks left and the woman walks right. 'Fifty thousand Euros?' Rosie thinks. 'Is there a story here?'

chateau /ʃæ'təʊ/ a big old house in France or Switzerland where a rich person lives

dangerous that can kill you

bridge people can go across a river on this

Rosie goes after the woman. 'Where's she going?' Rosie thinks. 'And who is she?'

Suddenly, the woman stops and looks back. She looks at Rosie for a second or two, then goes into a house.

Rosie goes to the house. '"Julia Yardley",' she reads. 'She's an **art dealer**. Art dealers **buy** and **sell** pictures. Perhaps the man on the river bus is going to buy a picture. But why is that dangerous?'

'Perhaps he's going to **steal** a picture!' Rosie thinks, suddenly. 'But what can I do?'

JULIA YARDLEY
Fine Art Dealer

London · Paris · New York

art dealer a person who has a shop with expensive pictures in it

buy to give money for something

sell to take money for something

steal to take something without asking

READING CHECK

Choose the right words to complete the sentences.

a Rosie Doyle is a journalist.
She must find . . .
- **1** ☐ fifty thousand Euros.
- **2** ☑ a big story.
- **3** ☐ Julia Yardley.

b She wants to . . .
- **1** ☐ see a film.
- **2** ☐ visit a chateau.
- **3** ☐ visit New York.

c She goes there by . . .
- **1** ☐ car.
- **2** ☐ plane.
- **3** ☐ river bus.

d She listens to . . .
- **1** ☐ Julia Yardley and Lezardo.
- **2** ☐ Pierre Valmy and Lezardo.
- **3** ☐ Julia Yardley and Pierre Valmy.

e They talk about . . .
- **1** ☐ a big story and London.
- **2** ☐ pictures and Paris.
- **3** ☐ money and Venice.

f Rosie goes after . . .
- **1** ☐ Lezardo.
- **2** ☐ Julia Yardley.
- **3** ☐ Pierre Valmy.

WORD WORK

Use the words in Big Ben to complete the sentences on page 7.

a That man is a killer. Be careful. He's *dangerous*.

b I want to .... those shoes in the window. How much are they?

c 'There are a lot of cars on this road. How can we get across it?'
'Look! There's a .... We can walk over that.'

d I read *The Times* every day. Which .... do you read?

e That picture is by Picasso. It's .... a lot of money.

f 'It's raining. What can we do today?'
'I've got an .... Let's watch TV at home.'

g That old woman can't see it, but that boy's .... money from her bag.

h We don't use our old TV. Let's .... it and get some money for it.

i 'What's the .... today?'
'England are playing France at football this evening.'

j He reads a lot in his work because he's an ....

GUESS WHAT

What happens in the next chapter? Read the sentences and write *Yes* or *No*.

a We learn more about Rosie. ....

b We learn more about Lezardo's work. ....

c We learn more about Julia Yardley's work. ....

d We see Pierre Valmy's home. ....

Two nights later, on a **mountain** in Switzerland, Roger Lezardo **skis** across the **snow**. It is after midnight. In front of him is a big chateau.

Lezardo **breaks** the **lock** on some doors and goes into the chateau.

mountain a big hill

ski to go over snow fast on long flat pieces of wood

snow something soft, cold and white

break to make one thing into two things when you hit it

lock this makes a door stay closed

Very quietly, he goes **upstairs**. He sees a door in front of him. 'That's Valmy's bedroom,' Lezardo thinks.

He goes into the room. Valmy is in bed, **asleep**. 'Get up, old man!' Lezardo says. 'Who – who are you?' Valmy asks.

Valmy sees the **gun** in Lezardo's hand. 'Get the **drawing**, Valmy,' Lezardo says.

'How do you know about–?' Valmy begins to ask.

'It doesn't matter,' Lezardo says. 'Get it!' Valmy gets a paper from the **safe** – a paper with a drawing on it.

---

upstairs to the upper part of a house

asleep sleeping

gun a person can fight with this

drawing a picture made with a pen or pencil

safe a box with a lock where you put important or expensive things

In a different room, a man gets out of bed. He is Hans, Pierre Valmy's **servant**. 'What's that noise?' he says. 'Who's talking? Is it **Monsieur** Valmy?'

In Valmy's bedroom, Lezardo takes the paper from the old man. Then he **ties** him to a chair.

He looks at the drawing and laughs. 'A million Euros for this little drawing?' he says. 'You **art collectors** are **crazy**.'

Lezardo leaves the chateau with the drawing in his bag.

Hans finds Monsieur Valmy. 'Go after him!' Valmy shouts. 'Take the **snowmobile**!' 'Yes, monsieur,' says Hans. 'And you call the **police**, monsieur.'

---

servant a person who works for someone rich

Monsieur /məs'jə/ Mr, in French

tie to stop someone moving with a rope

art drawings and pictures

collector a person who like to buy and have lots of things of one kind

crazy not thinking well

snowmobile a car that can go across snow

police they find people who do something bad

Hans quickly gets the snowmobile and goes after Lezardo. Lezardo skis down the mountain.

Lezardo sees Hans on the snowmobile behind him.

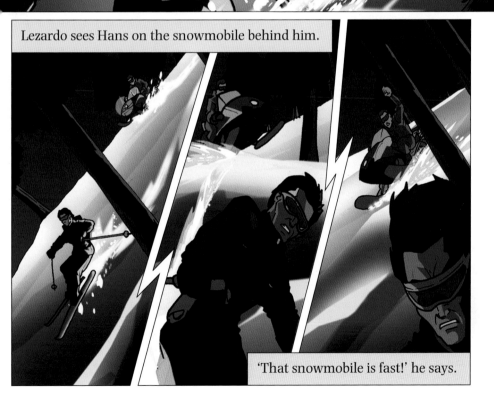

'That snowmobile is fast!' he says.

READING CHECK

Are these sentences true or false? Tick the boxes.

		True	False
a	Lezardo visits Pierre Valmy's house.	☑	☐
b	Pierre Valmy is a young man.	☐	☐
c	Pierre Valmy lives in Paris.	☐	☐
d	Lezardo takes a drawing from Valmy.	☐	☐
e	The drawing is worth a million Euros.	☐	☐
f	Hans works for Lezardo.	☐	☐
g	Lezardo puts Valmy's drawing in his bag and goes.	☐	☐
h	Valmy goes after Lezardo.	☐	☐

WORD WORK

1 Find sixteen words from Chapter 2 in the snow.

2 Use the words from Activity 1 to complete these sentences.

a I can open this door easily. The ......lock...... isn't working.

b That bottle is very old. Be careful with it and don't .... it.

c He's got lots of beautiful pictures in his house because he's an art ....

d I like it when it's cold and there's .... on all the trees and houses.

e She can .... down hills very fast.

f Watch that man. He's got a .... in his hand and he can kill you with it.

g 'Oh, no! That woman has got my bag with all my money in it.'

'Quick! Call the ....!'

h Everest is a very high ....

i The children are .... in bed so don't make a lot of noise.

j Her room isn't down here. It's ....

k I don't want to take all this money with me. Let's put it in the hotel ....
before we go out.

l This .... is by Leonardo da Vinci and it's worth a lot of money.

m She wears flowers in her hair and she doesn't wear shoes. She's ....

n They don't do any work in the house. Their.................. do it for them.

o She can't run away because he's .... her to a tree.

p I like studying .... because I like looking at beautiful pictures.

GUESS WHAT

**What happens in the next chapter? Choose the correct words to complete
the sentences.**

a Hans gets Lezardo.   Lezardo gets away.

b Rosie sees Valmy   Lezardo on TV.

c Valmy's drawing is by Leonardo da Vinci.   Pablo Picasso.

d Rosie goes to the police.   Venice.

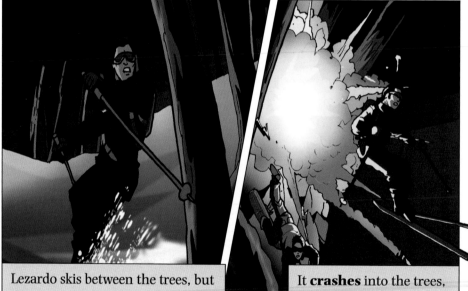

The snowmobile is getting nearer and nearer. 'What can I do?' Lezardo thinks.

Lezardo sees some trees in front of him. 'Wait!' he thinks. 'I can get through there!'

Lezardo skis between the trees, but the snowmobile can't **follow** him.

It **crashes** into the trees, and Lezardo **escapes**.

follow to go after something or somebody

escape to get away

crash to hit something and stop suddenly

'The owner of the chateau is Pierre Valmy.'
the news reader says. 'The Picasso drawing
is worth half a million Euros, perhaps more.'

'Valmy? I know that
name!' Rosie thinks. 'But
where . . .? Yes! From the
man on the river bus!'

Pierre Valmy is talking on
the TV now.
'The **thief** has the Picasso
drawing,' he says. 'But
what can he do with it?'

'I know,' Rosie says excitedly. 'He can give it
to Julia Yardley in Venice tomorrow at two
o'clock. And get fifty thousand Euros! The
thief is the man on the river bus!'

thief (*plural* **thieves**) a person who
takes things without asking

15

'Do I go to the police?' Rosie thinks.

'No. You go to the police *after* you get your big story, Rosie Doyle,' she says. 'Perhaps you're wrong. Perhaps it's a different man. Go to Venice and see!'

Rosie gets the next plane to Venice.

The next day, Rosie is on a **gondola** in Venice.

She gets off the gondola at the Rialto Bridge. 'Nearly two o'clock,' she thinks. 'Where are they?' She sits in a **café**, has a coffee, and waits.

gondola you can go across the water in this in Venice

café you go here to have a drink and something to eat

READING CHECK

Choose the correct words to complete the sentences.

a Lezardo skis between two (trees) houses .

b The snowmobile can can't go after him.

c Lezardo gets doesn't get away.

d Rosie is eating breakfast and watching the news a film on TV .

e She remembers the name Valmy Lezardo from the river bus.

f Valmy Rosie knows about Julia Yardley, Venice and the fifty thousand Euros.

g Lezardo Julia Yardley is an art thief, Rosie thinks.

h Rosie wants to go to the police before after she gets her big story.

i Rosie goes to Venice that day the next day .

WORD WORK

Use the words in the TVs to complete the sentences.

a Can you take a photo of us in this gondola? We want to remember everything about this week in Venice when we go home.

lano
dog

wolf
lo

b You go first and I can _ _ _ _ _ _ you.

see
pac

c How can we _ _ _ _ _ _ from this building? There is a killer with a gun at the front door and I can't open the back door.

srach

d Careful! You're driving very fast. Don't _ _ _ _ _ into the car in front of us.

fehit

e That boy is a _ _ _ _ _ . He takes money from people's school bags when they aren't looking.

f Are you hungry and thirsty? Let's have a sandwich and a coffee in that _ _ _ _

GUESS WHAT

What happens in the next chapter? Tick three sentences.

a ☐ Lezardo meets Julia Yardley at the Rialto bridge.

b ☐ Julia gives fifty thousand Euros to Lezardo.

c ☐ Lezardo gives the Picasso drawing to Julia.

d ☐ Rosie gets the drawing.

e ☐ Rosie speaks to the police.

f ☐ Lezardo and Julia speak to Rosie.

FOUR

Some minutes later, Julia Yardley arrives at the Rialto Bridge. 'There she is!' Rosie thinks. 'But where's the man?'

Lezardo isn't far away. He's watching Rosie.
'Why is that woman watching Julia Yardley?' he thinks. 'Does she know something?'

Rosie suddenly sees the man from the river bus. He's meeting Julia Yardley on the bridge.

Lezardo gives Julia Yardley a **package**.
'Is that the Picasso drawing?' Rosie thinks.

package something that you take with you in some paper

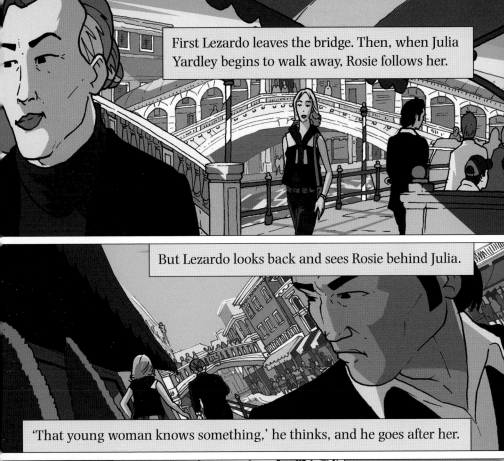

First Lezardo leaves the bridge. Then, when Julia Yardley begins to walk away, Rosie follows her.

But Lezardo looks back and sees Rosie behind Julia.

'That young woman knows something,' he thinks, and he goes after her.

Rosie follows Julia Yardley to a big hotel. Julia goes in but Rosie waits in the street.
'Now I can phone the police,' she says.

But Lezardo is behind Rosie now and he **grabs** her phone. 'No, you don't!' he says. 'What—?' Rosie begins.

From the hotel, Julia Yardley sees Roger Lezardo with Rosie in the street. Lezardo has Rosie's arm in his hand and she can't escape. 'What's happening?' she thinks. 'Wait! I know that young woman's face?' She goes out of the hotel again.

Now Julia is with Lezardo and Rosie. Lezardo pushes Rosie into a dark **alley** opposite the hotel. Julia follows them.
'Do I know you?' Julia asks Rosie, and she looks into Rosie's face. 'Ah, yes. Now I remember! Outside my London office, on Monday! Who are you?'
'Aaagh! My arm! You're **hurting** me!' Rosie cries.
'OK, OK! My name's Rosie Doyle. I – I'm a journalist.'

grab to take suddenly

alley a small street

hurt to do something bad to someone

'What do you know?' Lezardo asks. 'Be careful. I don't want to hurt you, but I have a gun in my **pocket**.'

'I know . . . I know about the drawing,' Rosie says. 'I know about Valmy.'
'How do you know?' Julia asks.

Rosie tells them about the London river bus.
'What can we do with her?' Julia asks Lezardo.
'Leave her with me,' Lezardo says. And he smiles **nastily**.

pocket the place in your coat where you can put things

nastily in not a nice way

READING CHECK

Put these sentences in the correct order. Number them 1–8.

a ☐ Rosie follows Julia.

b ☐ Lezardo leaves the bridge.

c ☐ Lezardo gives something to Julia.

d ☐ Julia arrives at the Rialto Bridge.

e ☐ Julia speaks to Rosie.

f ☐ Lezardo speaks to Rosie.

g ☐ Lezardo takes Rosie's phone.

h ☐ Julia goes into her hotel.

WORD WORK

Use the words in the water to complete the sentences on page 25.

a 'Have you got a pen?'
'Yes, I've got one in my shirt …pocket….'

b Don't ……………… the sandwiches. Take them slowly.

c I don't walk down that ……………… late at night. It's dark and nobody usually goes there.

d This ……………… is for you. It's from Oxford. What's in it?

e Please say sorry nicely, not ……………… .

f Don't sit on your little sister. You're ……………… her.

GUESS WHAT

What happens in the next chapter? Tick the boxes. Yes No

a Julia phones an art collector. ☐ ☐
b Julia gives Lezardo five thousand Euros. ☐ ☐
c Rosie phones the police. ☐ ☐
d Lezardo and Rosie go to Julia's hotel room. ☐ ☐
e Lezardo takes back the painting from Julia. ☐ ☐
f Rosie ties Julia to a bed. ☐ ☐
g Rosie ties Lezardo to a chair. ☐ ☐

CHAPTER FIVE

'What are you going to do?' Julia asks. She is **frightened**. Lezardo is a dangerous man. 'Don't ask questions,' Lezardo tells her. 'Phone your collector. I want my money soon.'

'Tomorrow,' Julia tells him. And she goes into the hotel.

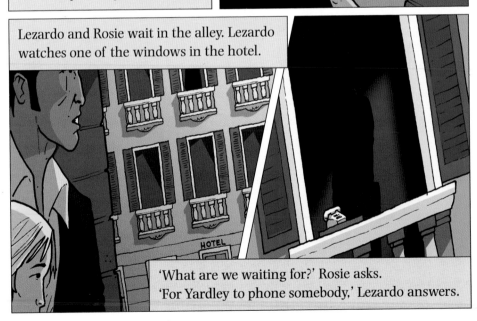

Lezardo and Rosie wait in the alley. Lezardo watches one of the windows in the hotel.

'What are we waiting for?' Rosie asks.
'For Yardley to phone somebody,' Lezardo answers.

frightened afraid

Five minutes later, Rosie sees Julia Yardley on a hotel **balcony**. Julia picks up a black book from the table and goes into her room.
'She's phoning. Now we go in,' Lezardo says. 'And don't run away! Remember the gun in my pocket!'

Lezardo gives some money to the man at the hotel desk.
'Well, Salvatore?' he says.
'She is in her room,' the man at the desk tells him. 'And now she's making a phone call.'

'Right. Who's she phoning?' Lezardo asks.
'Wait a minute,' Salvatore says, and he **picks up** the phone on his **desk** and listens.

'Giovanni Piano,' Salvatore says to Lezardo quietly.
Lezardo smiles. 'So she's selling to him – one of the most important collectors in Italy. I know him.'

balcony a place at the front of a building upstairs where you can stand and look out or sit in the sun

pick up to take in your hand

desk a table where you can pay for a room or ask hotel workers things

Salvatore puts down the phone. 'She's meeting him at four o'clock,' he tells Lezardo. 'At the Café Antonella.' Lezardo looks at his watch. 'There's not much time,' he says. 'What's her room number?'
'301,' Salvatore says.

'Giovanni Piano is crazy about collecting,' Lezardo says. 'He buys important **paintings** and drawings, and he asks no questions.'
'What are you going to do?' Rosie asks.

He laughs. 'I'm going to get back that Picasso drawing,' he says. 'Then I'm going to sell it to Giovanni Piano and get half a million Euros, not fifty thousand!'

Lezardo **knocks** on the door of room 301.

Julia opens the door and sees Lezardo's gun. 'What – what are you doing?' she says. She is frightened.

painting a coloured picture

knock to hit strongly

When they are in the room, Lezardo finds the drawing in Julia's **case**. He grabs it. Then he says, 'You two are going to stay here – quietly.' To Rosie he says, 'I'm going to come back for you later.' He smiles nastily again.

'Tie her to the bed,' Lezardo tells Rosie. Rosie looks at his gun and ties Julia to the bed.

Then Lezardo ties Rosie to a chair. After ten minutes, he is ready to leave with the drawing. 'See you later,' he tells Rosie and Julia.

case a big bag

ACTIVITIES

READING CHECK

Correct the mistakes.

a Julia phones an important Italian ~~police officer~~. *art collector*

b Lezardo gives some drawings to Salvatore.

c Lezardo listens to Julia's phone call with Piano.

d Julia is meeting Piano at two o'clock at the Café Antonella.

e Lezardo wants a million Euros for the drawing from Julia.

f He goes to room 103.

g He takes the drawing from Julia's safe.

h Salvatore ties Julia to the bed.

i Lezardo ties Rosie to a table.

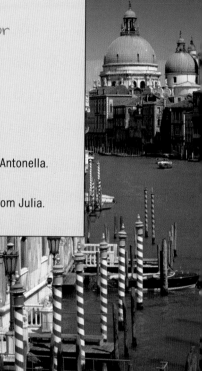

WORD WORK

1 Find six more words from Chapter 5 in the word square.

a	c	p	a	i	n	t	i	n	g	s
v	a	r	e	b	a	l	c	o	n	y
d	s	p	i	c	k	s	u	p	u	d
f	e	p	u	u	n	e	k	d	n	e
f	r	i	g	h	t	e	n	e	d	s
y	x	c	z	i	i	k	n	o	c	k

2 Use the words from Activity 1 to complete the sentences.

a There are lots of . *paintings*.. by Picasso in this art book.

b When it's hot I like to sit on my hotel .... in the sun.

c Look at that big dog! Help! I'm .... of dogs.

d I've got lots of important papers in my .... now. I'm taking them to work.

e When you arrive at a hotel, you must speak first to the man or woman at the front .... and get your room number.

f Please .... on the door before you open it and come in.

g My mother always .... my things when I leave them on the table.

GUESS WHAT

What happens in the next chapter? Tick one box.

a ☐ Rosie and Julia escape.

b ☐ Lezardo gets a million Euros from Giovanni Piano.

c ☐ Giovanni Piano phones the police.

d ☐ Lezardo escapes from the police.

SIX

After Lezardo leaves, Rosie **tries** to move her arms and legs. 'Perhaps . . . I can get out . . . on to the . . . balcony,' she thinks. She begins to move her chair.

Rosie gets her chair out on to the balcony. There is a newspaper on the table on the balcony. Rosie tries to knock it down to the street.

After some time, she knocks the newspaper off the table. It **falls** into the street and some people see it.

A young man sees the newspaper, then he looks up and sees Rosie. He runs to the hotel.

try to want to do something but not to do it well

fall to go down quickly

Some minutes later, the young man arrives at room 301 with the hotel **manager**.

The young man **unties** Rosie and the hotel manager unties Julia.
'My name is Bernardo,' the young man tells Rosie. 'Are you OK?'
'Yes, I'm OK,' she says. Then she tells the hotel manager, 'Phone the police! Tell them, "Go to the Café Antonella".'

Rosie tells Bernardo and the hotel manager about the Picasso drawing and Giovanni Piano. The hotel manager phones the police.

manager a person who watches the work of other people

untie to take off ropes that tie someone or something

Then he speaks to Rosie, Julia and Bernardo. 'The police are going to the Café Antonella,' he says. 'But they want to ask **Signora** Yardley some questions, too.'

'I'm going to the Café Antonella,' Rosie says. She looks at her watch. 'But there isn't much time.'

'We can go in my **boat**, Miss . . .!' the young man says. 'My name's Rosie,' Rosie says. 'OK! Let's go!'

At the Café Antonella, Lezardo waits for Giovanni Piano.

Giovanni Piano arrives some minutes later.

'Who are you?' he asks Lezardo. 'Where's Signora Yardley?' 'Forget Signora Yardley,' Lezardo tells him. 'Here's the drawing.' 'It's beautiful,' Piano says. 'I must have it!'

Signora /sɪnˈjɔrə/ Mrs, in Italian

boat you go across water in this

Suddenly, the two men see a police boat on the **canal**. Then Lezardo sees Rosie in Bernardo's boat. He gets up quickly.

More police arrive in the street. Lezardo looks at them, then at the police boat. It's very near now.

'You!' a policeman shouts at Lezardo. 'Stop!' But Lezardo runs to Bernardo's boat.

canal a river that people make

Lezardo gets onto Bernardo's boat. He knocks Bernardo into the canal.

Now Lezardo drives the boat away – fast!

Lezardo tries to get away from the police. It is not easy with gondolas and more boats on the canal.

Suddenly, there's a gondola in front of them, the boat **turns** quickly, and Rosie falls into the water! She **swims** to the gondola.

turn to go to the right or the left

swim to go through the water moving your arms and legs

Now Rosie is in the water by the gondola. Bernardo's boat crashes into a bridge and starts to **sink**. Lezardo falls into the water.

The police get Rosie out of the water first. Then they get Lezardo. 'Have you got the Picasso drawing?' Rosie asks a policeman. 'Yes, **thanks to** you,' he says.

The police take Rosie back to the hotel. Bernardo is waiting for her. 'Well, I've got my big story,' Rosie says. 'That's going to the editor of *The Record* tonight!' 'Are you a journalist?' Bernardo asks. 'Yes,' Rosie says.

'Er – can you stay in Venice for a day or two more, Rosie?' Bernardo asks. Rosie looks at him. 'He's nice,' she thinks. 'And I can send my story to the editor from here by **email**.'

'Yes, perhaps I can,' she says, and she smiles.

sink to go down in water

thanks to because of

email words that you send from computer to computer

ACTIVITIES

READING CHECK

Match the two parts of these sentences.

a Rosie knocks . . .

b Bernardo unties . . .

c Rosie tells Bernardo and the hotel manager . . .

d The hotel manager . . .

e Lezardo waits for Piano . . .

f Piano wants to have . . .

g Lezardo takes . . .

h The police get . . .

i In the end Rosie gets . . .

1 about the drawing.

2 at the Café Antonella.

3 Rosie.

4 Lezardo and the drawing.

5 phones the police.

6 a newspaper into the street.

7 her big story.

8 Bernardo's boat.

9 the Picasso drawing.

WORD WORK

1 Find words from Chapter 6 in the boats.

knignis
a s inking

mwis
b s _ _ _

inuet
c u _ _ _ _

langilf
d f _ _ _ _ _ _

ginytr
e t _ _ _ _ _

lacan
f c _ _ _ _

nurt
g t _ _ _

raagnem
h m _ _ _ _ _ _

skhatn ot
i t _ _ _ _ _ _ _ _

liema
j e _ _ _ _

2 Use the words from Activity 1 to complete the sentences.

a. I'm sorry but the hotel .manager.. is writing an .... now.

b. We're .... Can you ....?

c. I'm .... to .... you.

d. Oh no! That little girl is .... into the ....

e. .... you, Mr Holmes, we have got the thief!

f. When you get to the village shops, ... left and the hotel is on your left.

PROJECT A *Paintings*

1 **Complete the description of the picture by Picasso with the words in the box. Use a dictionary to help you.**

> *at the bottom   at the top   in the background*
> *in the foreground   on the left   on the right*
> *there are   there's*

1 .... we can see a market. **2** ....
we can see old building and the sky. **3** .... and left there
are vegetable shops **4** .... we can see two horses and a
dog. **5** .... a man in red on the white horse's back.
6 .... of the picture we can see some clouds in the sky and
on the the right-hand side of it **7**.............................. some birds on a roof.
8 .... of the picture we can see the street and some rubbish.

2 Look at the picture of part of Venice by Canaletto. Complete the table with the words from the box. Use a dictionary to help you.

> *a small brick bridge   buildings   clouds   dark water*
> *gondolas   bright blue sky   people walking   reflections*
> *the Grand Canal   the Rialto Bridge*

1 In the foreground	....
2 In the background	....
3 On the right	....
4 On the left	....
5 At the top	....
6 At the bottom	....

PROJECT B   *Police Interviews*

1 Complete this dialogue with Julia Yardley's words from the box.

> *At the Rialto Bridge Hotel.   I'm 40.   I'm an art dealer.*
> *In shops in London, Paris and New York.*
> *In a flat in London.   Julia Yardley   No, I don't.*
> *Yes, I do. He's an old friend.   American.*

Police Officer: What's your name?

Ms Yardley: 1 ....

Police Officer: What nationality are you?

Ms Yardley: 2 ....

Police Officer: How old are you?

Ms Yardley: 3 ....

Police Officer: Where do you live?

Ms Yardley: 4 ....

Police Officer: Where do you work?

Ms Yardley: 5 ....

Police Officer: What's your job?

Ms Yardley: 6 ....

Police Officer: Where are you staying in Venice?

Ms Yardley: 7 ....

Police Officer: Do you know Giovanni Piano?

Ms Yardley: 8 ....

Police Officer: Do you know Pierre Valmy?

Ms Yardley: 9 ....

2 Write the police officer's words in this interview with Giovanni Piano.

Police Officer: 1 ....
Giovanni Piano: Giovanni Piano.
Police Officer: 2 ....
Giovanni Piano: I'm 50.
Police Officer: 3 ....
Giovanni Piano: Italian
Police Officer: 4 ....
Giovanni Piano: In an apartment in Rome.
Police Officer: 5 ....
Giovanni Piano: I run a spaghetti business.
Police Officer: 6 ....
Giovanni Piano: In an office in Rome.
Police Officer: 7 ....
Giovanni Piano: In the Saint Mark's Square Hotel
Police Officer: 8 ....
Giovanni Piano: No, I don't.
Police Officer: 9 ....
Giovanni Piano: Yes, I do. She's an old friend.

3 Now write a police interview with Roger Lezardo.

Police Officer: ....
Roger Lezardo: ....
Police Officer: ....
Roger Lezardo: ....
Police Officer: ....
Roger Lezardo: ....
Police Officer: ....
Roger Lezardo: ....
Police Officer: ....
Roger Lezardo: ....
Police Officer: ....
Roger Lezardo: ....
Police Officer: ....
Roger Lezardo: ....
Police Officer: ....
Roger Lezardo: ....
Police Officer: ....
Roger Lezardo: ....

GRAMMAR CHECK

Present Simple: affirmative and negative

We use the Present Simple to talk about habits and facts which are always true, or true for a long time.

Art dealers buy and sell pictures.

To make most Present Simple affirmative verbs we use infinitive without to. With he/she/it we add –s or –es.

Rosie goes to the River Thames and waits for the river bus.

To make most Present Simple verbs negative, we use don't (do not) + infinitive without to. With he/she/it we use doesn't (does not) + infinitive without to.

She doesn't get up early on Sundays.

1 **One piece of information in each sentence is incorrect. Change the word in italics and correct the sentences.**

a Rosie wants to find a *picture*.

   Rosie doesn't want to find a picture. She wants to find a big story.

b Julia and Lezardo talk on a *train*.

   ....

c Julia Yardley buys *books*.

   ....

d Valmy lives in *Venice*.

   ....

e *Lezardo* works for Valmy.

   ....

f Rosie sees Valmy *in the newspaper*.

   ....

g *Julia* and Giovanni Piano meet at a café.

   ....

h Lezardo takes Bernardo's *car*.

   ....

i The police catch *Rosie and Bernardo*.

   ....

GRAMMAR

GRAMMAR CHECK

Articles: a/an, the

We use the indefinite articles **a/an** with singular nouns to talk about a thing or idea for the first time.

'A big story! That's not easy to find,' thinks Rosie. 'But a film? That's a good idea.'

We use **an** with singular nouns that start with a vowel sound.

Lezardo and Rosie wait in an alley. (One of many alleys.)

We use the definite article **the** with singular and plural nouns to talk about things the speaker and listener know from before.

The job isn't easy. And it's dangerous. (We already talked about it.)

Two o'clock at the Rialto Bridge. (There is only one Rialto Bridge.)

2 Complete the emails with *a*, *an*, or *the*.

From: julia@wanobee.net.uk

To: lazardo.r@yeeha.co.it

I have a) ...an... interesting job for you. Can you steal b) .... picture for me? It's c) .... drawing. d) .... Italian collector wants to buy e) .... drawing, and he doesn't ask any questions!

From: lazardo.r@yeeha.co.it

To: julia@wanobee.net.uk

I'm interested in f) .... job, but what is g) .... picture and where is it? Is it in h) .... museum, i) .... art gallery or j) .... house? And what about k) .... money?

From: julia@wanobee.net.uk

To: lazardo.r@yeeha.co.it

It's l) .... drawing called *Mother and Child,* by Picasso. m) .... art collector called Pierre Valmy has got it. He lives in n) .... chateau in o) .... mountains in Switzerland. Valmy sleeps in p) .... upstairs room. q) .... drawing is in r) .... safe. Meet me in London on Tuesday: take s) .... usual water bus at three o'clock. We can talk about t) .... money when we meet.

GRAMMAR CHECK

Imperatives

We use imperatives to tell people what to do or to give them advice. We use the infinitive without to for affirmative imperatives.

Give me the drawing!

We use negative imperatives to tell people not to do something. Negative imperatives start with do not or don't + infinitive without to.

Don't be late!

3 Complete the sentences with the words in the box.

open	get	stop	don't run	leave	go
don't go	don't try	~~take~~	don't ask	phone	give

a ..Take.. the afternoon off.

b .... up, old man!

c .... the safe and .... the drawing to me!

d .... away! Remember the gun in my pocket.

e .... questions. Go back to your hotel.

f .... your collector! I want my money soon.

g See you later. And .... to escape!

h .... to the Café Antonella!

i Hey, you! ....!

j .... to London tomorrow.

4 Who says the things in Exercise 3? Match these sentences with the sentences in 3.

1 Lezardo tells Valmy this.   ..*b*... and ....

2 The hotel manager says this to the police.   ....

3 Lezardo says this to Julia and Rosie.   ....

4 The police shout this to Lezardo.   ....

5 Lezardo says this to Julia.   .... and ....

6 Rosie's editor says this to her.   ....

7 Lezardo says this to Rosie.   ....

8 Bernardo says this to Rosie.   ....

GRAMMAR CHECK

Present Continuous: affirmative and negative

We use the Present Continuous to talk about things that are happening now.

For the Present Continuous affirmative and negative, we use the verb be + the –ing form of the verb.

⊕ *Rosie is eating breakfast in her London home.* *You're hurting me!*

⊖ *Signora Yardley isn't meeting Giovanni Piano because she's in the hotel.*

With most short verbs that end in consonant + vowel + consonant, we double the final consonant and add –ing.

sit – sitting   get – getting   stop – stopping

With verbs that end in consonant + –e we lose the final e and add –ing.

give – giving   phone – phoning   take – taking

5 Look at the pictures and complete the text with the affirmative or negative form of the verbs in the boxes.

wait	~~sit~~	hold	look	drink	watch	read	think

Julia a) ...*is sitting*... at a table in a café, but she
b) .... a coffee and she c) .... at the
beautiful buildings – she d) .... about the Picasso
drawing and she e) .... for Lezardo. Rosie is in the
café too. She f) .... a newspaper, but she
g) .... it. She h) .... Julia Yardley.

listen	talk	phone	say	tell

Julia is upstairs in her room. She's
i) .... an art dealer called Giovanni
Piano. They j) .... about the picture.
Julia k) .... when she can meet
Piano. At the hotel reception desk, Salvatore
l) .... to the phone call and he
m) .... Lezardo all about it.

GRAMMAR CHECK

Present Continuous: questions

For Present Continuous questions, we use the auxiliary verb be and the –ing form of the verb. Information questions begin with a question word, such as *what, where, who,* or *why.*

Who's she phoning?   What are we waiting for?

For Yes/No questions, we reuse the verb be in the answer.

Is Lezardo working for Julia?   Yes, he is.

6 Use the words to make questions. Then match the questions with the answers 1–8.

a where / Rosie / go? .... *Where's Rosie going?* .... ⑤

b why / she / wear / a coat? .... ☐

c what / she / think / about? .... ☐

d what / the people behind her / do? .... ☐

e they / take / photos? .... ☐

f who / sit / in front of her? .... ☐

g what / they / talk / about? .... ☐

h Rosie / listen / to them? .... ☐

1 No, they aren't.

2 Lezardo and Julia.

3 Yes, she is.

4 They're looking at buildings.

5 ~~She's going to the cinema~~.

6 The people in front of her.

7 Because it's a cold day.

8 Money.

GRAMMAR CHECK

Reference words

We use reference words when we don't want to repeat the same word.

'The thief has the Picasso drawing,' he says. 'But what can he do with it?'

7 **Write these reference words in place of the words in brackets in the text. Use some of them more than once.**

she	him	it	them	he	they	his	there

Pierre Valmy is an art collector. a) ......He.... (Valmy) collects important pictures from all over the world. Lezardo wants to steal a drawing from b) .... (Valmy). c) .... (The drawing) is in d) .... (Valmy's) safe. Lezardo wakes Valmy up in the middle of the night and tells e) .... (Valmy) to open the safe. Valmy opens f) .... (the safe) and gives Lezardo the drawing because g) .... (Lezardo) has got a gun.

Lezardo wants to fly to Venice and sell h) .... (the drawing) to an art dealer called Julia for €50,000. i) .... (Julia and Lezardo) are meeting j) .... (in Venice) tomorrow, and k) .... (Julia) is bringing money for Lezardo. But Rosie knows about Julia and Lezardo and l) .... (Rosie) is going to Venice because she wants to follow m) .... (Julia and Lezardo).

GRAMMAR CHECK

Time phrases

We use time phrases to talk about when events happened, and to show the order of these events.

The next day, Rosie is on a gondola in Venice.

Some minutes later, Julia Yardley arrives at the Rialto Bridge.

After ten minutes, he is ready to leave with the drawing.

Rosie suddenly sees the man from the river bus.

8 Complete the story about Rosie with the time phrases in the box.

some time	before nine	suddenly	first	next morning
then	minutes	a few days later	after three hours	

a) A few days later, Rosie says goodbye to Bernardo at the airport.

b) .... in a plane, she arrives in London. The c) ...., she gets up early and goes to work. She arrives at the newspaper offices just d) .... o'clock, puts her bag on the table and sits down in her chair. After a few

e) ...., she looks at the room. Where are all her things? f) ....,
she gets a call on the phone. She picks it up. It's her friend Melanie.

'Hey Mel. How are you?' says Rosie.

'I'm fine,' says Melanie, 'But why are you in your old room?'

At g) ...., Rosie doesn't understand.

'Your story is really big, Rosie. It's the biggest story of the year!' says Melanie. Just

h) ...., Rosie sees the newspaper on the table: *Journalist of the Year, Rosie Doyle.*

After i) ...., Melanie says. 'Come upstairs to your new room! You're an editor now.'

Rosie puts down the phone, smiles and opens her bag. She gets the photo of Bernardo from her bag. 'A new man and a new job in one week,' she thinks. 'Now that's a big story.'

▌▌DOMINOES Your Choice▐▐

Read *Dominoes* for pleasure, or to develop language skills. It's your choice.

Each *Domino* reader includes:
- a good story to enjoy
- integrated activities to develop reading skills and increase vocabulary
- task-based projects – perfect for CEFR portfolios
- contextualized grammar activities

Each *Domino* pack contains a reader, and an excitingly dramatized audio recording of the story

If you liked this *Domino*, read these:

Changing Places
Alan Hines
Hal works at the zoo every day and his life isn't exciting – until he meets Tim.
Tim is a movie star. He has a difficult life, and he is unhappy – until he meets Hal.
But when they meet, and agree to change places, interesting things start to happen. And, by changing places, the two men learn what is truly important in their lives.

Sinbad
Retold by Janet Hardy-Gould
Sinbad the sailor spends many years at sea. He visits strange countries, meets some strange people and some very frightening animals. He is sometimes rich, sometimes poor . . . and always in danger. But all the time he is learning from his adventures, until finally he returns home to Baghdad, an older and wiser man.

	CEFR	Cambridge Exams	IELTS	TOEFL iBT	TOEIC
Level 3	B1	PET	4.0	57-86	550
Level 2	A2–B1	KET-PET	3.0-4.0	–	390
Level 1	A1–A2	YLE Flyers/KET	3.0	–	225
Starter & Quick Starter	A1	YLE Movers	1.0–2.0	–	–

You can find details and a full list of books and teachers' resources on our website:
www.oup.com/elt/gradedreaders